a Catholic Christmas

KATHLEEN M. CARROLL

FOREWORD BY SISTER ROSE PACATTE, F.S.P.

D1410108

ST. ANTHONY MESSENGER PRESS
Cincinnati, Ohio

Cover and book design by Mark Sullivan
Cover image © Chiff | Dreamstime.com

Quotes are taken from the English translation of the
Catechism of the Catholic Church for the United States of America (indicated as
CCC), 2nd ed. Copyright 1997 by United States Catholic Conference—Libreria
Editrice Vaticana. Used by permission.

Scripture passages have been taken from *New Revised Standard Version Bible*, copyright
©1989 by the Division of Christian Education of the National Council of the
Churches of Christ in the U.S.A., and used by permission. All rights reserved.

LIBRARY OF CONGRESS CATALOGING-IN-PUBLICATION DATA
On file at the Library of Congress

ISBN 978-1-61636-163-1

Copyright ©2011, Kathleen M. Carroll. All rights reserved.

Published by St. Anthony Messenger Press
28 W. Liberty St.
Cincinnati, OH 45202
www.AmericanCatholic.org
www.SAMPBooks.org

Printed in the United States of America.

Printed on acid-free paper.

11 12 13 14 15   5 4 3 2 1

Contents

FOREWORD by Sister Rose Pacette, F.S.P., *v*

INTRODUCTION, *1*

CHAPTER ONE: THE ORIGINS OF CHRISTMAS
Roots in Rome, 5

CHAPTER TWO: THE LITURGICAL YEAR
Keeping Sacred Time, 19

CHAPTER THREE: THE FEAST OF ST. ANDREW
First Things First, 33

CHAPTER FOUR: THE FEAST OF ST. NICHOLAS
The Real Santa Claus, 41

CHAPTER FIVE: THE IMMACULATE CONCEPTION
Mary, Our Mother, 49

CHAPTER SIX: THE FEAST OF ST. LUCY
Let There Be Light, 61

CHAPTER SEVEN: THE NATIVITY
The Center of the Christmas Season, 71

CHAPTER EIGHT: THE FEAST OF ST. STEPHEN
Begin With the End in Mind, 81

CHAPTER NINE: THE FEAST OF THE HOLY FAMILY
Celebrating the Domestic Church, 91

CHAPTER TEN: THE FEAST OF THE EPIPHANY
East Meets West, 99

CHAPTER ELEVEN: THE BAPTISM OF OUR LORD
A New Beginning, 109

NOTES, 115

BIBLIOGRAPHY, 117

Foreword

D1411625

One of my favorite Christmas movies is *Millions*, a film made in 2004 that takes place in Widnes, a suburb of Liverpool, England. Nine-year-old Damian's mother has died, and his father has moved him and his brother Anthony to a new house to start afresh. Damian is grieving, but his faith is strong. He takes the large boxes from the new appliances and makes a kind of hermitage out in the back yard, near the train tracks. His playhouse is in stark contrast to their new neighborhood and the secular Christmas decorations and noise of the world outside.

The story develops from the improbable notion that the U.K. is changing its currency from the pound to the euro. The deadline for turning in old currency is a few days away, right after

Christmas. One day, while Damian is in his hermitage, bags of the outgoing cash crash through the roof. The money is stolen, but Damian thinks it is from God. He can only think of doing good with it, helping the poor as Christ has taught, while Anthony wants to spend it, his dad wants to pay off his credit cards, his dad's girlfriend wants a vacation, the government wants to burn it, and the thieves want their money back.

The boys attend Catholic school, and as Christmas draws near a woman speaks to the students about collecting money to dig wells for clean drinking water in Africa. Damian has found his mission, just in time for Christmas. He will bring water, living water, to the poor.

The film is very Franciscan in its orientation because it chooses poverty—or "enoughness"—and charity for one's neighbor over money and possessions. This gentle parable is filled with saints: St. Peter, St. Francis, St. Clare, St. Joseph, St. Nicholas of Myra, the Ugandan martyrs. They look after Damian and his family and visit the boy who has an encyclopedic knowledge of their stories. In fact, if you look closely, you can tell Damian has been reading a book about the saints in his cardboard castle. He recognizes each of them immediately, except St. Francis who witnesses without saying a word. Damian greets them by giving the dates they were born and died. He is so thoroughly comfortable in the presence of the saints, and his innocence is so transparent, that it beckons the yearning child in each of us.

Damian is always looking for his mother so he asks St. Nicholas, as he does each of the saints, if they have seen "St. Maureen—she's new."

A Catholic Christmas is Kathleen Carroll's second Christmas book, a companion to *A Franciscan Christmas*, which imagines to life the figures of the crèche, from Jesus, Mary and Joseph, to the magi, and even the musicians, just like the first live nativity scene created by St. Francis of Assisi in 1223.

A Catholic Christmas is populated with holy characters and saints, too, as their feasts occur on the liturgical calendar. They prepare us through the Scriptures and the witness of their lives during Advent, to join those who will gather at the crèche during the always too brief Christmas season culminating with the baptism of Our Lord.

Carroll's comfortable tone, like that of Damian's familiar chats with the saints, invites the curious and the catechist to take a stroll through history to look at how the Church frames the liturgical calendar year in sync with nature and culture. Most of all, she reassures readers that despite secularism and materialism, the real

Christmas, in the care of the Church, has stood the test of time and trial and will continue to do so.

Carroll adds a reflective dimension to each chapter, and often a catechetical or pastoral application, so that no matter how the reader engages in *A Catholic Christmas*, he or she will find food for thought while preparing for the celebration of the miracle of the Christ's birth.

In *Millions*, Damian does finally find his mother, and they chat for five minutes before she has to go. He asks her if she is a saint, and she tells him that the criteria are rather strict. A miracle is needed. He asks her, "What's your miracle?" "Why, don't you know, Damian? It's you."

In the movie, Damian and his family crawl through the narrow confines of Damian's cardboard tunnel, symbolizing the stranglehold that possessions can have on us, and they emerge ready to be born again. They transport to Africa to celebrate a new life with villagers as fresh clean water springs from a new well that the money has made possible. Carroll's book concludes the Advent and Christmas seasons with the Feast of the Baptism of Our Lord, recalling our life in Christ, ready to live Ordinary Time in extraordinary "enoughness" and charity.

Although the etymology of Widnes, the name of the town where *Millions* takes place, is rather vague, it sounds a lot like "witness," a Christmas witness. This book is just that.

—*Rose Pacatte, F.S.P.*

Introduction

*"But when the time had fully come, God sent forth his Son, born of
a woman, born under the law, to redeem those who were under the
law, so that we might receive adoption as sons." This is "the gospel of
Jesus Christ, the son of God": God has visited his people. He has ful-
filled the promise he made to Abraham and his descendants. He acted
far beyond all expectation—he has sent his own "beloved Son."*[1]

These days, more than ever, there seems to be a war on Christmas.
Every autumn, local courts fill with cases about public displays
of the Nativity scene and banners that wish the public a "Merry
Christmas" instead of the more generic "Happy Holidays." Schools
scramble to maintain their tradition of a Christmas pageant without

running afoul of the need for inclusivity. The media amplifies the conflict by reporting on every lawsuit, complaint, and school memo that touches on the topic, however tangentially. If you'd just landed on Earth, you'd think there was a vast secular campaign to erase all vestiges of the religious aspect of Christmas.

In these pages, I'd like to offer another perspective—a minority report, if you will. I'd like to tell a little bit about the history of Christmas and how our Western celebration of it has developed over the centuries. I'd like to share some of what I've learned about the origins of some of our most cherished traditions. And, most of all, I'd like to share the good news that even if every last foot soldier of evil were in fact on a mission to destroy Christmas, they'd have no chance.

A Catholic Christmas looks at the Christmas season through the lens of the liturgical year. This perspective allows us to see the holiday as part of the evolving story of the life of Jesus on earth, and to understand how the events we celebrate each week at Mass connect to the big picture of our lives as faithful Christians. In both liturgy and the liturgical calendar, we find the blueprint for who we are and what we are to do as disciples of Christ and modern-day bearers of the covenant made between God and the Israelites, our ancestors in faith.

I invite you to make this Christmas a Catholic Christmas by learning how much we owe to the Church in keeping the ancient traditions of our faith alive. I hope you will celebrate the feasts of the liturgical year, the feasts of the saints, and the season itself with a new sense of appreciation for the riches available to us in the history of our faith.

And, mostly, I hope you will discover that, despite the weakness inherent in any organization made up of frail and fallen humans, you needn't worry about the "war on Christmas." The Church has been competently handing on the faith for two millennia now, and the "gates of hell shall not prevail against it" (Matthew 16:18, *ESV*).

CHAPTER ONE

The Origins of Christmas

ROOTS IN ROME

The faith of the first community of believers is based on the witness of concrete men known to the Christians and for the most part still living among them. Peter and the Twelve are the primary "witnesses to his Resurrection," but they are not the only ones—Paul speaks clearly of more than five hundred persons to whom Jesus appeared on a single occasion and also of James and of all the apostles.[1]

*W*e all know the story of Jesus' birth in Bethlehem. In Scripture, each Gospel writer tells the story a little differently. Matthew begins his Gospel with "An account of the genealogy of Jesus the Messiah…" before setting down his telling of the nativity story. Luke gives the most detailed and comprehensive account of the birth of Jesus, with great emphasis on the Marian aspect of the story.

Mark and John both begin with Jesus' encounter with John the Baptist, skipping over the story of Jesus' life prior to the events that led to his public ministry. John's Gospel, in fact, presents a mystical account of Jesus' entry into the world with the words: "In the beginning was the Word, and the Word was with God, and the Word was God." For most of us, however, the Gospel stories, our traditions, and even a few elements contributed by pious and not-so-pious authors have merged together into one big story about the birth of Jesus.

We know that Jesus was conceived by the Virgin Mary and born in a stable at Bethlehem in the humblest of surroundings. We know that wise men from the East followed a star to honor the newborn king, that Joseph had dreams that helped him protect the child and his mother. Our songs and traditions incorporate some or all of these elements into our celebrations and occasionally embellish a detail or invent new stories altogether. "The Little Drummer Boy," for example, will not be peeking at you from the pages of any Bible.

Christmas wasn't quite "Christmas" that first year, though. It was simply Jesus' birthday. While his mother and earthly father and a few foreign gentlemen had an idea that this was no ordinary child, most people were not attaching the word "Christ" to him just yet.

So while Jesus was growing up, he and his family didn't celebrate Christmas. Their family life centered on the holy days of the Jewish faith they all embraced. Though the Gospel writers don't always go to great pains to spell this out for us (there is really very little about Jesus' childhood in Scripture), it is evident in the stories about the presentation in the Temple (remember Simeon and Anna?) and in the finding in the Temple (after Jesus' three-day disappearance). We can't say with certainty that Mary and Joseph didn't celebrate Jesus' birthday but the word *birthday* appears just once in the Bible

(Genesis 40:20), to refer to the pharaoh's birthday.

When did the celebration we call Christmas really start? About three hundred years after the birth of Jesus.

The Early Church

In its infancy, Christianity was not a popular religion. Believers met secretly to share the Scriptures, celebrate the Eucharist, and encourage one another in the faith. Once Christianity was seen as its own religion and not simply one branch of Judaism (as the Romans first understood it), it lost the special privilege the Empire had long granted to Jews—to worship their one God to the exclusion of all others. Even to the exclusion of the Roman gods. Even to the exclusion of the emperor himself.

Although sacrificing to pagan gods and worshiping the emperor were no more palatable to the early Christians than to their Jewish neighbors, they were not exempt from the law. The persecutions of the first centuries of the faith stem from this basic incompatibility. Failure to worship the emperor was treason, and the punishment for treason was death—often a spectacular and gruesome death. Some of the early martyrs were thrown to the lions, some were crucified. One of the goriest tales we have comes from the Roman historian Tacitus. He relates that Nero had Christians rounded up, covered in tar, and slowly burned alive to provide light and ambience for his lavish garden parties.

People who knew these martyrs were stunned by the horror of the persecutions, but even more impressed that people would sooner succumb to such a dreadful and certain fate than deny their faith in Jesus. Rather than having the deterrent effect the Romans had hoped for, the persecutions actually helped to spread the faith. Church father Tertullian famously described this phenomenon by saying, "The blood of the martyrs is the seed of the church." Memorials were set up in honor of these certain saints, and believers would gather on the anniversary of their deaths (which were thought of as their "births" into eternal life) to celebrate the Eucharist.

Once Christianity was legalized by the Emperor Constantine with the Edict of Milan in AD 313, these feast days could be celebrated publicly. This happened slowly, at first (you can imagine why). As believers began to share their faith, they realized that many of them had developed slightly different traditions. The days on which saints' feasts were celebrated did not always align. Some saints were known only in their local communities, while some had become famous throughout the Church.

Pope St. Julius I, whose papacy ran from 337 to 352, worked to make the celebrations of the universal Church more uniform. Saints' feasts became part of the Church calendar, locally in the case of saints who were known only in a small area, and universally in situations were the saint's fame had spread throughout the Church. And there was one last detail left to Julius: establishing the date of Christmas.

When Was Jesus Born?

During the time of Julius I, Christians were still arguing (sometimes violently) about whether Jesus was divine, and it is no surprise to learn that they did not always agree on the details of his life, either. One of these details was the exact date of Jesus' birth. The Bible doesn't mention a date, so there was no single authority that could end the controversy.

Several branches of the Church celebrated the day on different dates, each of which had its own rationale. Some tried to identify the astronomical event that led the Magi to Bethlehem and extrapolated the date from there. Others had ancient traditions that led them to celebrate a given date. Several of these dates clustered around late December and early January (though some differed wildly). It fell to Pope Julius to rule finally on the date when the Western Church would celebrate Christ's birth. His choice was December 25.

This was not an arbitrary choice. In many regions, this date corresponded closely with when the feast was already celebrated. There was also a sound correlation with another feast on the liturgical calendar (which we'll discuss more later in this book). But the single most persuasive reason for settling on late December was more political—there was a longstanding Roman celebration already being observed around that date.

The Roman Origins of Christmas

Despite such disastrous missteps as the destruction of the Temple, the crucifixion of Jesus, and the use of humans as party lanterns, the Roman Empire had a vibrant culture. One of the biggest holidays celebrated by the Roman people (often to the chagrin of rulers from Augustus to Caligula) was Saturnalia. Saturn was the god of sowing, among other things, so there was some rationale for appealing to him during the shortest days of the year (the winter solstice falls on December 21 or 22) in hope that the sun might return again and provide life-support for that agrarian culture.

Catullus called the Saturnalia "the best of days" (Catullus 14.15) for its deep roots in the celebration of the winter solstice and the rebirth of light and mirth in the heart of winter. The festival dates varied through the course of Roman history, but began as the feast day of Saturn (December 17) and his wife, Ops (December 19), both ancient Roman fertility deities. Saturn was the god of agriculture (merging later with the Greek god Cronos) while Ops was the goddess of plenty and mother earth. During the Roman Empire the ever-popular festival was extended to seven days, from December 17 through December 23.

> In each Roman home, the Master might wait on his own servants and one of the slaves was commonly chosen as *Saturnalicius Princeps* (Master of the Saturnalia), who could order others around in a complete reversal of roles. On the final day (December 23), everyone exchanged small gifts including *sigillaria* (small, special-event pottery dolls) for the children and *cerei* (small candles) for adults.[2]

Although the cultural observance of Saturnalia may have influenced the decision to set the date for Christmas on December 25, celebrating the birth of Christ in the middle of winter makes perfect sense. Christ is the intersection of all things. He brings the light into the darkness—when better to remember this than during winter's longest nights? He brings eternity into time—how better to be mindful of this than to see the traces of ancient practices in our modern celebrations?

What better moment to reflect on both the brevity and great expanse of time than at the close of one year and the beginning of the next? And Christ is the intersection of East and West—the sky-gazing mystics of the East came to honor him; his birth occurred in Bethlehem because his parents traveled there to be counted for the Roman census. To situate the celebration of his birth between the ancient date of January 6, used in the Eastern Church, and the Roman winter festival combines the best of both.

The selection of December 25 as the date for Christmas is a profound reminder to us that ordinary things do not somehow "corrupt" what is holy. On the contrary, the Incarnation elevated this material world—and especially our human nature—to a new level of sanctity. The Church does not minimize Christmas by locating it on the date of a pagan feast; rather, it elevates that feast and the people who celebrated light and life and family in the centuries before Christ. It remembers that, though they did not have the same opportunity to believe in Jesus that we have today, they knew and honored what was best about humanity—the very humanity for whom Christ did not hesitate to die.

Jesus might have been born in the middle of May, for all we know from Scripture, but I agree with Pope Julius I—the quiet of winter is the best time to remember the occasion.

How does Christmas remind you of the sanctity of ordinary things? This Christmas, as you decorate a common tree with even-more-common tinsel, consider how the birth of Jesus has changed everything.

CHAPTER TWO

The Liturgical Year

KEEPING SACRED TIME

The economy of salvation is at work within the framework of time, but since its fulfillment in the Passover of Jesus and the outpouring of the Holy Spirit, the culmination of history is anticipated "as a foretaste," and the kingdom of God enters into our time.[1]

I attended Catholic schools for a number of years—a couple in grade school, six days in high school (but, my, they were six memorable days), and nine years and counting in post-graduate work. I've worked in Catholic publishing long enough to spot a heresy a mile away and to avoid giggling at the mention of St. Homobonus. But, I will confess, there are subtleties in the liturgical calendar that I despair of ever grasping.

First, there is Ordinary Time. This I get. Whenever we're not celebrating some huge event, it's Ordinary Time. The Church and the priest are usually decked out in green. The tricky part is that we don't call it Ordinary Time because it's ordinary (though it does make it a mite easier to remember). The *ordinary* comes from the Latin word *ordinal*, and is used to indicate that it is counted time. Beyond this, it gets harder. Fr. Tom Richstatter has managed to give a succinct overview:

> The liturgical year is the arrangement of the Church's celebrations of the various events in the life of Christ and

the mysteries of our faith throughout the year. From the time of the apostles, Christians have gathered together on the first day of the week, the day of the Resurrection, the Lord's Day, to celebrate the Lord's Supper. In the course of time, these weeks were organized into two "seasons": Lent/Easter and Advent/Christmas. Between the seasons of Lent/Easter and Advent/Christmas we have two periods of non-seasonal time, "Ordinary Time," so named for the Latin *ordo*, "the order of things." This sequence of Sundays and seasons is punctuated by celebrations of various feasts of the Lord, the Blessed Virgin Mary and the saints.[2]

Why is the liturgical year important? First, as noted in the introduction, the fact that we have Christmas at all and that we have it when we do is a direct result of the liturgical calendar. We go to Mass on Sundays and begin our season of repentance on Ash Wednesday and all manage to show up to celebrate Easter on the same day because the Church makes it so. The mention of Easter is particularly germane because, in many ways, it's how the liturgical calendar got started.

Calendars are so much a part of our everyday lives that it's easy to overlook their importance. When most people lived closer to the land and had to be more attuned to its rhythms, knowing the date could be a matter of life and death. Most ancient cultures had a calendar of some sort. Some were based on the moon, which conveniently goes through the same phases every month (or more accurately, for whose phases we have coined the term *month*). Others were solar (like our present-day Gregorian calendar) and there are about a half-dozen variations on these two.

In an agrarian society, if you could not know with certainty when the spring equinox occurred, you would not be able to sow your crops late enough to avoid the last frost and early enough to harvest before the weather turned cold again. If yours was a seafaring culture, celestial navigation required knowing where the sun was rising and what constellations would be visible in the sky. The ancients took their calendars pretty seriously. So, too, the Church.

The Importance of Easter

While some might find the Church's appointment of December 25 as the date for Christmas a bit lacking in historical vigor (more on that in chapter three), there can be no such complaint over its zeal to determine the date of Easter. The very same Council of Nicaea that had defining the nature of Christ on its agenda (and you thought *your* meetings were important), determined that Easter would fall on the first Sunday after the first full moon after the vernal equinox.

In case you do not have a Bible within arm's reach, I offer here a few reminders about the Scriptural descriptions of Easter. As you will remember, the resurrection was preceded by the crucifixion, which was preceded by the Last Supper. You might also remember that Jesus dropped a few hints about his impending death at that table, only to be met with confusion and arguments from his disciples.

This Last Supper, then, wasn't a soiree they all put together because they knew that Jesus would soon be taken from them. Why, then, were they all gathered for this feast? Because it was Passover, the Jewish holiday commemorating the exodus of the Chosen People from their slavery in Egypt. Passover was celebrated in the Jewish month of Nisan, on the first full moon after the vernal equinox.

Since Jesus rose from the dead on a Sunday (which is why Sunday is now the Lord's Day, though Jews celebrate the Sabbath on the seventh day—Saturday), the date of Easter becomes a bit more understandable. So we know that Jesus rose on Sunday, and we know that it was the Sunday immediately after Passover. So far, so good. The problem now becomes: How do you know when it's the first Sunday after the first full moon after the vernal equinox? At first, Christians simply took their cues from their Jewish neighbors. That arrangement soon lost its luster, as J.L. Heilbron describes in *The Sun in the Church: Cathedrals as Solar Observatories:*

> Unfortunately, only the rabbis could say when Nisan began. Early Christian communities had to apply to the leaders of a rival church to learn when to celebrate their principle feast. The ignominy of this procedure, and the difficulty of a timely dissemination of the result as the church spread, forced the bishops into arithmetic. They sought a way to determine their own Nisan and to compute the dates of Easter far in advance.[3]

After a brief outline of just how the bishops went about it, Heilbron sighs, "Their line of thought may be expressed easily with the help of algebra they did not possess. God knows how they did it." Ultimately, for the Church, the cathedrals were the answer.

To set a date for Easter Sunday years in advance, and thus reinforce the Church's unity, popes and ecclesiastical officials began to rely on astronomers, who pondered over old manuscripts and devised instruments that set them at the forefront of the scientific revolution.

The Church—that very same Church whose mistakenly low opinion of Galileo gets all the press—devoted massive amounts of financial and social support to the study of astronomy for over six centuries, from the recovery of ancient learning during the late Middle Ages into the Enlightenment. And, like many patrons, the Church wanted something practical in return for its investment: mainly the improvement of the calendar so Church officials could more accurately establish the date of Easter.

In its scientific zeal, the church adapted cathedrals across Europe, and a tower at the Vatican itself, so their darkened vaults could serve as solar observatories. Beams of sunlight that fell past religious art and marble columns not only inspired the faithful but provided astronomers with information about the Sun, the Earth and their celestial relationship. Among other things, solar images projected on cathedral floors disclosed the passage of dark spots across the Sun's face, a blemish in the heavens, which theologians once thought to be without flaw. Over the centuries, observatories were built in cathedrals and churches throughout Europe, including those in Rome, Paris, Milan, Florence, Bologna, Palermo, Brussels and Antwerp.[4]

Thus, having solved the "crisis" of Easter, the Church was able to put the rest of the liturgical calendar to rights without much difficulty.

The liturgical year starts with Advent, the season in which we anticipate Christmas, the commemoration of Jesus' birth. According to the liturgical calendar, Christmas is an entire season, not just a single day, beginning with the first Sunday of Advent and continuing to the Feast of the Baptism of Our Lord, celebrated on the Sunday following the Epiphany.

When the Christmas season ends, we move into a brief period of Ordinary Time, before our preparation for Easter begins on Ash Wednesday, the first day of Lent. As we have seen, the date for Easter can shift dramatically and, as a result, the same is true for Lent and Ash Wednesday.

Holy Week begins on Palm Sunday (the Sunday before Easter) and continues to Holy Thursday, when we remember the Last Supper. Starting with the evening liturgy on Holy Thursday and ending with evening prayer on Easter Sunday, this time is a season unto itself, called "Triduum." The Easter season then continues until Pentecost Sunday.

Pentecost is celebrated on the seventh Sunday after Easter Sunday (it originally fell fifty days—the word *Pentecost* means *fifty*—after the beginning of Passover) and commemorates the descent of the Holy Spirit upon the apostles. The following Sunday is Trinity Sunday. It is followed by the Feast of Corpus Christi, which ushers in another long season of Ordinary Time until Advent begins again.

If you pay attention to the liturgical seasons, you'll begin to see lots of cycles in the Church. In addition to this grand yearly scheme, you'll notice that your local parish offers Masses and devotions at different times of the week, for different reasons. If you look into the Church's prayer (the Divine Office) you'll find a prescribed way for praying at all hours of the day—from the pre-dawn Matins to the just-before-retiring Compline. In all of these efforts, the Church is carrying on Christ's work of sanctifying everything, especially time.

The Liturgical Celebration of Christmas

When our ancestors in faith remembered their local martyrs, it was usually with a Mass on their feast day, and these holy feasts developed names to reflect the tradition. The same is true for other celebrations in the Church calendar—candles were blessed on Candlemas, the archangel Michael was honored on Michaelmas (his birthday, too, being tricky to pin down), and St. Martin of Tours was remembered on Martinmas.

And, just as the birthdays of the saints were not always known, the Church often selects other dates to remember its holy men and women. For example, Pope John Paul II was born in May and died in April, but his feast date has been set on October 22—the day he became pope. Now, we might perhaps see some confusion in Octobers to come over this decision and, centuries or millennia hence, we might lose the exact dates of John Paul II's reign as pope, but his feast day will remain the same.

So, whether you believe there is enough historical reason to celebrate the birth of Jesus on the 25th of December, the Church makes it easy: A feast is whenever the Church says it is. That we celebrate the birth of Jesus at all is a gift of the Church. And that we have the opportunity to celebrate it at Mass is the Church's greatest gift.

The best way to celebrate Christmas (and, I promise you, the real reason the Church insists on it—not those wrinkled bills you toss in the basket [though I'm sure those are appreciated as well]) is by attending Mass. Whether it's on Christmas Eve, at Midnight Mass, or Christmas Day itself, the celebration of the Eucharist will best remind you of just how miraculous it is that Christ came to be with us on Christmas and continues to be with us at Mass. If you didn't find the gift you wanted under the tree this year, go to Mass. Jesus has a better one for you.

What about the Christmas season most reminds you of the great gift of the Incarnation? This Christmas, find some quiet way to share that joy and wonder with someone who needs it.

CHAPTER THREE

The Feast of St. Andrew

FIRST THINGS FIRST

From the beginning of his ministry, he "called to him those whom he desired; ....And he appointed twelve, whom also he named apostles, to be with him, and to be sent out to preach." From then on, they would also be his "emissaries" .... In them, Christ continues his own mission: "As the Father has sent me, even so I send you." The apostles' ministry is the continuation of his mission; Jesus said to the Twelve: "he who receives you receives me."[1]

*A*dvent always begins on the Sunday closest to the feast of St. Andrew. As recounted in the Gospels of Matthew and Mark, when Jesus hears that John the Baptist has been arrested, he travels to Galilee to begin his ministry. Within the span of a few verses, Jesus has four disciples, Andrew among them.

> As he walked by the Sea of Galilee, he saw two brothers, Simon, who is called Peter, and Andrew his brother, casting a net into the sea—for they were fishermen. And he said to them, "Follow me, and I will make you fish for people." Immediately they left their nets and followed him. As he went from there, he saw two other brothers, James son of Zebedee and his brother John, in the boat with their father Zebedee, mending their nets, and he called them. Immediately they left the boat and their father, and followed him. (Matthew 4:18–22)

We are more familiar with the other apostles called to follow Jesus on that day. Simon, Andrew's brother would become St. Peter, upon whom the Church was founded. James and John—the "Sons of Thunder"—have more prominent roles in the Gospels. These three are distinguished among the disciples as having a closer relationship with Jesus. They accompany him to the mountain where the Transfiguration occurs, and travel with him to the Garden of Gethsemane, to share in his sorrow. But by connecting Andrew to the beginning of Advent (the beginning of the liturgical year), the Church is inviting us to see the "firstness" of Andrew.

The Orthodox tradition further emphasizes this "firstness" of Andrew by the name *Protokletos* ("first called"). Tradition (and the Gospel According to John) claims that Andrew was a disciple of John the Baptist. When John tells his followers, "Behold, the Lamb of God," Andrew immediately follows Jesus: "One of the two who heard John speak and followed him was Andrew, Simon Peter's brother" (John 1:40). When he next speaks with his brother Simon, he claims that he has found the Messiah. We know that Peter often gets the credit for being the first of the apostles to proclaim that Jesus is the Christ, but John's Gospel suggests that he got the idea from his brother.

Andrew also seems to have given his brother the inspiration for his martyrdom. Peter was famously crucified upside down, at his own request, because he felt unworthy to be killed in the same way as Jesus. Andrew was martyred seven years earlier on an X-shaped cross (called a *saltire*), for the same reason. The cross of St. Andrew is the X that appears on the flag of Scotland, of which he is patron, and is the source of the X shape that appears in the more familiar Union Jack.

The most important thing we can learn from the firstness of St. Andrew is what he did first and what he put first. He was called with the first disciples and, immediately leaving both his community and his livelihood behind, clearly put Jesus first. Letting Andrew introduce us to the Advent season and the new liturgical year provides us with the same introduction to Jesus that St. Peter had.

Just as Andrew introduced Peter to Jesus, some ancient traditions remember the feast day of St. Andrew by promising to give young women some introduction to their future husbands. In central Europe, one practice was to pour hot candle wax through a keyhole into cold water. The resulting shape was interpreted to give some indication of the future groom's occupation. Another tradition was for a young woman to throw a clog over her shoulder; if it landed facing the door, she would be married within that Church year.

A more contemporary suggestion for celebrating St. Andrew's Day is to make a list of the firsts in your life. You can wander through your memories for a few enjoyable moments, but try to focus on the firsts in your faith life. Do you remember your first confession? I know I struggled to find some sins to tell the priest (I rarely have that problem these days). What about your first Communion? Break out the photo if you have one and try to remember how you felt on that day.

This Christmas, in honor of the first feast day of Advent, take some time to consider what you place first in your life. If it's not Jesus, take a hint from Andrew.

CHAPTER FOUR

The Feast of St. Nicholas

THE REAL SANTA CLAUS

By canonizing some of the faithful, i.e., by solemnly proclaiming that they practiced heroic virtue and lived in fidelity to God's grace, the Church recognizes the power of the Spirit of holiness within her and sustains the hope of believers by proposing the saints to them as models and intercessors. "The saints have always been the source and origin of renewal in the most difficult moments in the Church's history."[1]

*S*t. Nicholas of Myra lived and acquired his reputation for sanctity long before the Church began its formal process of beatification. He became recognized as a saint by a kind of popular acceptance.

Historians and hagiographers generally write that much of what is said about Nicholas is legend. In Nicholas's time there was no investigation and no authentication of claimed miracles before canonization took place. Attributing miracles and wonders to a person was an ancient way of expressing people's conviction about the holiness of the person, and enough to qualify them for sainthood.

You will still find Nicholas listed in the various dictionaries of saints, for example, *Dictionary of Saints*, by John Delaney, and Alban Butler's *Lives of the Saints*. And you will still find Nicholas listed in the Roman Calendar on December 6. There he is assigned an "optional memorial." In other words, churches and communities on that day may choose to celebrate either the liturgy in honor of St. Nicholas or the liturgy for a weekday in Advent.

Yet the legend of St. Nicholas has shaped much of the person of Santa Claus, and many of the traditions of the Christmas season. So, who was this man Nicholas? According to Butler's *Lives of the Saints*, Nicholas was born during the third century in what is now Turkey. He became a bishop at an early age, and was known throughout the region for his generosity and love of children. The Greek histories of the time note that he was persecuted and imprisoned for his faith during the reign of the Emperor Diocletian, and that he was present at the Council of Nicaea in AD 325.

One of the most popular stories about Nicholas tells of his generosity to a prominent citizen of Patara, near Myra. The man had lost all his money, and as such could not provide a dowry for his three daughters. As was sadly typical in the ancient world, women were entirely economically dependent on men. Without a dowry, women of that time could not marry, and might be sold into slavery. Legend has it that on three separate occasions, Nicholas tossed a bag of gold coins into an open window in the man's house, and the coins landed in shoes left by the fire to dry. Thus the man could provide dowries for his daughters and they were able to be married.

This legend led to the custom, popular in Germany, Switzerland and the Netherlands, of leaving one's shoes outside the bedroom door on the eve of December 6, in expectation of a small gift or coins. It is the basis for our modern-day custom of hanging stockings by the fire at Christmas. Incidentally, it is also the reason why pawnbrokers are often symbolized by three gold balls—Nicholas's gift "redeemed" those young girls as one might redeem a favorite watch from a pawn shop.

St. Nicholas was first brought to the New World first by the Vikings, who dedicated their cathedral to him in Greenland, and then by Columbus, who named a Haitian port for St. Nicholas on December 6, 1492. As the Americas became populated by Europeans from different countries, they brought their own customs and practices with them, including the traditions around St. Nicholas.

In the early 1800s, the character of St. Nicholas began to creep into a more secular symbol of Christmas, especially evidenced in 1823, by the publication of "A Visit from St. Nicholas," a poem attributed to Clement Moore. In this poem, St. Nicholas is described:

He was dressed all in fur, from his head to his foot,
And his clothes were all tarnished with ashes and soot;
A bundle of toys he had flung on his back,
And he looked like a peddler just opening his pack.

Quite a different depiction from the image of a Turkish bishop from the fourth century, who would have been arrayed in far more regal garb!

Whatever the historical basis of Nicholas of Myra, he has proved to be an enduring figure and symbol of the Christmas season. The elements of wisdom, generosity, and kindness found in his story provide an excellent model for us during this time of year. Santa Claus or St. Nicholas, jolly man or gentle giver, patron saint of children and of sailors, his legend mirrors the gifts we share in his name.

What are your earliest memories of Santa? When did you find out that he was not what you expected? This Christmas, remember the heroism of parents (perhaps even your own, or you yourself) who labor to offer a bit of magic and mystery to their children in celebration of Christ's birth. Ask yourself how you can be more saintly—and Santa-ly—this year.

CHAPTER FIVE

The Immaculate Conception

• DECEMBER 8 •

MARY, OUR MOTHER

The "splendor of an entirely unique holiness" by which Mary is
"enriched from the first instant of her conception" comes wholly from
Christ: she is "redeemed, in a more exalted fashion, by reason of the
merits of her Son." The Father blessed Mary more than any other
created person "in Christ with every spiritual blessing in the heavenly
places" and chose her "in Christ before the foundation of the world, to
be holy and blameless before him in love."[1]

*U*nless you're a zealous convert, or perhaps a catechist, this chapter is going to blow your proverbial mind. It touches upon two much-misunderstood beliefs of the Church—the Immaculate Conception and the infallibility of the pope.

In the nineteenth century, a fourteen-year-old French peasant girl named Bernadette was gathering firewood with her sister and a friend. Dawdling behind the other two as they returned home (they had to cross a stream and Bernadette did not want to ruin her stockings), Bernadette had a vision of Mary. At first, she did not know what she was seeing. She described a shining figure in white who asked her to return to the grotto of the appearances every day for the next two weeks. She told her family of the vision and they were not as supportive as might have been hoped. (In their defense, I have a teenage daughter and would also not be very enthusiastic about her meeting someone in the woods.) Bernadette persisted and did as the shining figure instructed. As the crowds gathered, that obedience had a cost. When the figure told Bernadette to drink from the spring, the crowds gasped to see the young girl digging with her fingers in the mud (there was no visible spring) and even swallowing the soggy earth. At length, a spring did appear.

When Bernadette asked this shining apparition her name, she was told only, "I am the Immaculate Conception." Bernadette repeated this to her parish priest but had no idea what it meant.

The Church authorities who took an interest in the mysterious occurrences at Lourdes (the site of Bernadette's grotto) were another matter. They knew precisely what was meant by that statement as, just four years previously in 1854, Pope Pius IX had declared as a doctrine of the Church that Mary had been conceived without original sin—an event the Church called "the Immaculate Conception." It had long been an accepted belief in the Church that Mary had always been sinless, but there had been countless controversies about just what this meant or how it occurred. In settling the controversy Pope Pius resorted to declaring the doctrine *ex cathedra*—a rather arcane bit of language indicating that he was stating this under the guidance of the Holy Spirit as pope, as the head of the Church, and as a matter of doctrine. Rather than quelling controversy, however, this stirred up a bit of its own.

No one, probably least of all the popes themselves, is comfortable with the idea that someone is infallible—incapable of being wrong. Thus, when Pius took the newly defined idea of papal infallibility for its first test drive (the doctrine was promulgated by the First Vatican Council in 1870), there was some resistance. The arguments against papal infallibility are legion and needn't be cataloged here, but it seems pretty evident that all humans are wrong some of the time. For anyone to state otherwise seems pompous at best and insane at worst.

However, consider the alternative. Christ established the Church to guide us all toward salvation. It was the Church that created, preserved, and propagated the Scriptures. It was the Church that preserved our many sacred traditions (have you ever seen the word "Trinity" in the Bible, for example?) to help us understand the faith that has been revealed to us. And it is the Church that has the duty of protecting the revealed "deposit of faith" (as theologians call it) for all generations to come. Certainly St. Peter could not have given us guidance on the proper Christian use of automobiles or the Internet. The letters of St. Paul don't mention Islam or how we should relate to it. And no Church leader today can predict how the world will change in the centuries to come. So since it is clear that the world changes in unexpected ways, and it is also clear that followers of Christ are expected to continue in the faith even in these new circumstances, would it make any sense at all for Christ to have left us without some certain guidance?

The Church says no. And, lest some suggest that this is because the doctrine of papal infallibility tends to the Church's advantage, I believe that it is simply because that is what makes sense. God has gone to extraordinary lengths to reveal the means of our salvation to us. Why would he allow that to simply fade into irrelevance when the world changes?

If the idea of papal infallibility still troubles you, please take a look at the *Catechism of the Catholic Church* where the purpose behind this doctrine and its meaning for us today is covered in exhaustive detail. In the meantime, it might help to know that the pope has spoken *ex cathedra* exactly twice—once to declare the doctrine of the Immaculate Conception, and once to declare the doctrine of Mary's assumption into heaven.

Now, back to Bernadette and the grotto. You have doubtless by now made the connection between St. Bernadette and Our Lady of Lourdes, as we now know her. You probably recall some stories about Bernadette's visions and about the hundreds of miraculous cures attributed to the waters of the now-famous spring at the grotto. But why, when asked, did Mary not give her name, instead saying, "I am the Immaculate Conception"?

If I have been at all persuasive on the topic of papal infallibility, you might reasonably infer that she was using this language to show some support for the poor, beleaguered holy father. But perhaps she wanted us to look a bit more closely at the doctrine he so recently proclaimed, which we will now do.

Ask ten Catholics what the Immaculate Conception was and nine will tell you that it means that Jesus was conceived while Mary was a virgin. (The tenth will tell you a long story about football.) While it is true that Jesus was conceived by, let's say, extraordinary means, this is not what the Immaculate Conception is all about.

Early Christians had a hard time understanding how Mary, a normal human woman, could conceive and bring forth Jesus, God-made-man. This wasn't because they lacked respect for women, or even because the whole virgin birth thing troubled them (it didn't). Rather, they could not understand how someone sinful—even someone only guilty of original sin, someone who had never committed an actual willful sin in her life—could possibly be worthy to bear the Savior. At the same time, the puzzlement went, if Mary wasn't guilty of even original sin, then she wouldn't need a Savior, would she? And we'd need a whole new set of theological principles to describe the special case of this one person.

The doctrine of the Immaculate Conception neatly solves this dilemma. It explains that, indeed, Mary was free from all sin—even the stain of original sin. But, far from meaning that she did not need Jesus, the doctrine explains that her sin was eliminated in anticipation of her cooperation with God in the Incarnation. If you see a bit of time-travel at work here, you're right. Well, sort of. God exists and works outside of time and so can do anything at anytime or even everything at once. It was only at the Incarnation that God broke into our world, into our understanding of time to live as one human man two thousand years ago.

One last item to clear up: Some are confused by the appearance of the feast of the Immaculate Conception just before Christmas. Wouldn't its date suggest that the two are related?

In fact, the Feast of the Immaculate Conception falls on December 8, exactly nine months before we celebrate the Feast of the Nativity of Mary—her birthday. Rather tidy, yes? And exactly nine months before Christmas, on March 25, we celebrate the Feast of the Annunciation, when the angel appeared to Mary to announce that she had been chosen to be the Mother of Our Lord.

It is helpful to deepen our understanding of Mary and the Church at the same time because, in a very real way, Mary is Mother of the Church and our mother as well. Students of Scripture point to

Jesus' words from the cross, telling the Beloved Disciple, "Behold, your mother," even as he tells Mary, "Behold, your son." By these words, Jesus tells all those left behind—and that includes us—that we still have each other. Mary has a world of children to look after and we have a heavenly mother to turn to.

Are there aspects of the faith that you still find puzzling or mysterious? This Christmas, resolve to spend the coming months unwrapping the gift of your faith by reading up on topics still beyond your understanding.

CHAPTER SIX

The Feast of St. Lucy

LET THERE BE LIGHT

Through the Holy Spirit we are restored to paradise, led back to the Kingdom of heaven, and adopted as children, given confidence to call God "father" and to share in Christ's grace, called children of light and given a share in eternal glory.[1]

*I*f you've ever seen a statue or picture of a young woman holding a plate on which rests two eyeballs, that would be St. Lucy. (Do an online image search for "St. Lucy" if you want in on this one.) Her life is not historically verifiable, yet she is mentioned in the Canon of the Mass and celebrated as a symbol of light in the darkness. She is also the patron of many eye conditions.

Butler's *Lives of the Saints* situates Lucy as being born in Syracuse, Sicily, to a wealthy nobleman and his wife. Her story contains a miracle; as a young woman, Lucy is said to have gone with her mother to the tomb of St. Agatha to pray for her mother's healing from a hemorrhage. As they prayed, her mother was healed, and in gratitude, Lucy vowed to remain a virgin. This did not sit well with the young man to whom she had been engaged at an early age, however, and he exposed her as a Christian to the Roman governor. The year was AD 304, the height of the persecutions of Diocletian.

Lucy was at first sentenced to prostitution and ordered to be taken to a brothel. Here legend tells that she was struck immovable, so much so that even when she was fastened to a team of oxen she could not be moved. A fire was then built around her and lit, but Lucy was not harmed. Finally, a soldier took his sword and pierced her in the throat; even then, she prophesied against her persecutor until she died. (Some accounts of her life have her surviving the throat-piercing and dying only after she was beheaded.)

There are a number of stories that account for the depiction of Lucy with her eyes on the plate. One says that her eyes, of a remarkable beauty, were gouged out by her persecutors; another that they were extracted by her fiancé. There is also a story that claims Lucy took out her own eyes so that they could not be admired by potential suitors. In any case, each of the stories notes that God restored her eyes to be even more beautiful than before. (This explains the fact that in depictions of St. Lucy holding the plate with eyeballs on them, her face is shown with eyes intact.)

Before the Gregorian reform of the Julian calendar in 1582, December 13 was the date of the winter solstice, the shortest day of the year. Since most of Lucy's life is constructed from legend and folklore, we might wonder if the supposed date of her death— December 13—was selected because of the connection between the shortest day of the year and Lucy's name, which has its roots in the Roman word *lux*, meaning "light." Dating back to ancient times, many customs honor both Lucy and the promise of light extending beyond the darkness of winter.

In northern Europe, the faithful would light "Lucy fires"—great bonfires—to burn through the night of her feast. People would throw incense on the fire, and play music to celebrate the start of longer days once again.

In Italy, several customs still persist in celebration of Lucy's feast. In Sicily, the practice is to abstain from wheat products on that day, in commemoration of St. Lucy's intervention during a famine in the sixteenth century. Instead, they eat a porridge-like dish called *cuccia*, made with ricotta cheese and sugar. Venetian gondoliers claim Lucy as their patron. If you've heard the folk song "Santa Lucia," especially popular with these canal-workers, you've heard a song in St. Lucy's honor.

But it is in Scandinavia where the feast day of St. Lucy borders on a national holiday. Each year on December 13 people in Sweden recall the legend of how Lucy wore candles on her head as she brought food to persecuted Christians hiding in the dark catacombs beneath the city of Rome. In commemoration, one of the daughters of the family dresses in a white robe with a red sash, and wears a garland on her head with candles in it. She brings coffee and a pastry called Lussekatt to the rest of the family while they are still in bed. Some areas of the United States celebrate some variation of this Swedish tradition, too.

An Essential Element of Christmas

The light that pierces the darkness of winter is a central symbol of a Catholic Christmas. Jesus is the light of the world. The birth we celebrate on Christmas day doesn't simply cast a nice light on those twenty-four hours. It changes everything.

One of the stories told of Satan's fall from heaven says that he was once the brightest star in the sky—named Lucifer for his brilliance. When human men and women were created and God revealed his plan to the angels that one day these mortals would be his own adopted sons and daughters, the reaction was mixed. Many of the angels accepted God's pronouncement and vowed to serve humanity as the Lord directed. But Lucifer—out of an abundance of devotion rather than jealousy—refused. "No, Father," he said. "I will serve only you."

If there were any truth to this legend, and if the Incarnation had never taken place, then (brace yourself) Satan was right. There is nothing about a race of upright hairless primates that would justify angelic subjugation. But once the light of Christ shines on to our circumstances, everything changes. We are not mere animals, not even mere angels in monkey-suits; the Lord has made real our adoption, given us the power to become his sons and daughters. In this light we outshine even that once-brightest star of heaven.

At Christmas, we celebrate the season with lights of every description—candles, tree lights, decorations on the house. Each seems to add its own charm to the special light of Christmas. But all these lights take on a deeper significance when we consider that first light that gives meaning to them all.

How are lights part of your holiday preparations? This Christmas, consider making a special effort to emphasize the holier lights—a candle in church or the sparkle in a child's eyes. How can you add to the light of the world?

CHAPTER SEVEN

The Feast of the Nativity

THE CENTER OF THE CHRISTMAS SEASON

Belief in the true Incarnation of the Son of God is the distinctive sign
of Christian faith: "By this you know the Spirit of God: every spirit
which confesses that Jesus Christ has come in the flesh is of God."
Such is the joyous conviction of the Church from her beginning
whenever she sings "the mystery of our religion":
"He was manifested in the flesh."[1]

*H*aving tackled some of the more obscure doctrinal niceties of the faith, we come to the relatively easy idea of Christmas. Whenever I walk myself through the basic tenets of the faith, this most familiar of ideas never fails to stun me. It is always an astonishment to me that Christians can contemplate the idea of the Incarnation and still show up to work or school the next day. You may find it quite a bit easier to accept the truth of this, but allow me to take you on a tour of my own thought process. It runs along these lines:

1. **God created you.** That one is pretty straightforward. You didn't create yourself, clearly. Your parents had a hand in it, sure, but if they were 100 percent responsible you would probably have turned out differently, yes? (If you are one of those rare persons whose parents think perfect, you may go on believing that they cooked you up in a Petri dish, if you like. The rest of this chapter will be here when they finally find fault with you.) Thus, out of

the, let's say, fifty bajillion possible combinations of human genes, social and cultural circumstances, physical and mental abilities and disabilities, and accidents of birth (to say nothing of accidents of conception), God put you together. You're welcome.

2. **God knows about you.** Once upon a time, during the Enlightenment, some otherwise very smart men thought that perhaps God was like a great cosmic clockmaker who built the universe, set it in motion, and then walked off to do other things. I believe they thought he had hobbies. Scripture offers another point of view, with the Lord saying to Jeremiah as he says to us all:

> Before I formed you in the womb I knew you,
> and before you were born I consecrated you. (1:5)

The Church is also very clear on this point:

> Although man can forget God or reject him, He never ceases to call every man to seek him, so as to find life and happiness. (*Catechism of the Catholic Church*, #30).

Thus, you are here and you are here on purpose.

3. God loves you. You'll have heard this one before. In fact, you've probably heard it so many times before that it has lost its meaning. So I'm going to ask you to just sit with that one for a while. I could offer you dozens of texts supporting this statement but I think that if you just ponder it for a while you will eventually be struck by the obviousness of it. And the unbelieveableness of it. All at once. Then, I'm afraid, I'm going to have to make it worse.

4. God became human. Not because it looked like all sorts of fun, I'm reasonably certain, but to help you really grasp point #3, above. You've seen this in a thousand stories. Romeo became an exile for Juliet (who did him one better by becoming temporarily dead for his sake); Arwen became mortal for Aragorn (this is a *Lord of the Rings* reference; ask your geeky friend.); Bella became a vampire for Edward's sake (this is a *Twilight* reference; ask any teenage girl.). You'd have to have a pretty big struggle with believing that God loves you if God was to persist in his, well, Godness while leaving you to muck about in your, well, youness. So he decided to do something quantumly less believable in the Incarnation, just to drive the point home. (There's far more incredible things further along in the story, but we'll leave off here for now.)

That's the big backdrop of the Nativity. If you're struggling with this (that means you're paying attention), it gets a bit harder still. The details are not what we might expect. God became human in a political backwater of the Roman Empire at a time when life wasn't easy for anyone. And he didn't become Julius Caesar's great-nephew, which would have been far more comfortable for him (to say nothing of Nero's garden torches). He was born to a young Jewish girl and her very confused husband, a couple so poor and in such dire straits that they made a crib for their son out of a manger. There he is, the God of all heaven and earth, in such a fragile body and in such delicate circumstances that a single misplaced hoof could end the story before it has fully begun. This is God expressing himself; God saying, "I love you. Really. *Really.*"

We celebrate the Nativity every year not because we really understand any of this (who could really understand any of this?), but because we have just wit enough to know that something truly important has happened. And each year when we celebrate it we try to get through the parts we grasp completely (Where is the green extension cord? How many strands of lights are you allowed to link together?) so we can spend a few moments simply flummoxed at what we don't grasp at all.

This, I believe, is the center of the Christmas season and the center of most of our faith experience—a great "Wow!" combined with a massive "What?" As long as we can hang on to both the wonder and the mystery, we'll be OK.

Do you have a hard time accepting God's love for you? This Christmas, consider someone who might have a hard time believing you love them. Then prove it.

CHAPTER EIGHT

The Feast of St. Stephen

BEGIN WITH THE END IN MIND

Martyrdom is the supreme witness given to the truth of the faith: it means bearing witness even unto death. The martyr bears witness to Christ who died and rose, to whom he is united by charity. He bears witness to the truth of the faith and of Christian doctrine. He endures death through an act of fortitude. "Let me become the food of the beasts, through whom it will be given me to reach God."[1]

Good King Wenceslas looked out,
On the Feast of Stephen,
When the snow lay round about,
Deep and crisp and even;
—"Good King Wenceslas"

*T*his popular Christmas carol is the first introduction for many people to St. Stephen and his feast day, celebrated on December 26. The words to the carol "Good King Wenceslas" tell the story of a tenth-century Bohemian king who looked out his door on the feast of St. Stephen, and "a poor man came in sight / Gathering winter's fuel."

The tale unfolds throughout the verses that follow. Wencelas asks his page about the man so he can help him. The page replies that the man lives quite a bit away, "by Saint Agnes' fountain." Wenceslas goes inside, gathers food and wine and logs for a fire, and sets out with his page for the place where the poor man lives. Along the way the page begins to succumb to the cold; "I can go no longer," he cries. But the king urges him forward: the heat rises from Wenceslas's footprints in the snow, and the page is warmed and able to continue.

The carol ends with these words:

> Therefore, Christian men, be sure
> Wealth or rank possessing
> Ye who now will bless the poor
> Shall yourselves find blessing.

While the carol honors Wenceslas, patron saint of the Czech Republic, it is a tribute to the spirit of St. Stephen, first martyr and one of the first deacons of the Church. For someone whose feast day is such an established part of the Christmas season, we know little about Stephen's life except that which is found in Acts of the Apostles, chapters six and seven. It is enough to tell us what kind of man he was:

> Now during those days, when the disciples were increasing in number, the Hellenists complained against the Hebrews because their widows were being neglected in the daily distribution of food. And the twelve called together the whole community of the disciples and said, "It is not right that we should neglect the word of God in order to wait on tables. Therefore, friends, select from

among yourselves seven men of good standing, full of the
Spirit and of wisdom, whom we may appoint to this task,
while we, for our part, will devote ourselves to prayer and
to serving the word." What they said pleased the whole
community, and they chose Stephen, a man full of faith
and the Holy Spirit. (Acts 6:1–5)

Thus Stephen became one of the first seven people chosen
as deacons of the Church. (The others are Philip, Prochorus,
Nicanor, Timon, Parmenas, and Nicolaus of Antioch. There will
not be a quiz.)

Acts says that Stephen was a man filled with grace and power,
who worked great wonders among the people. Certain Jews,
members of the Synagogue of Roman Freedmen, debated with
Stephen but proved no match for the wisdom and spirit with which
he spoke. They persuaded others to make the charge of blasphemy
against him. He was seized and carried before the Sanhedrin.

In his speech, Stephen recalled God's guidance through Israel's
history, as well as Israel's idolatry and disobedience. He then
claimed that his persecutors were showing this same spirit. "[Y]ou
are forever opposing the holy Spirit; just as your ancestors used to
do" (Acts 7:51b).

But filled with the Holy Spirit, he gazed into heaven and saw the glory of God and Jesus standing at the right hand of God. "Look," he said, "I see the heavens opened and the Son of Man standing at the right hand of God!" But they covered their ears, and with a loud shout all rushed together against him. Then they dragged him out of the city and began to stone him; and the witnesses laid their coats at the feet of a young man named Saul. While they were stoning Stephen, he prayed, "Lord Jesus, receive my spirit." Then he knelt down and cried out in a loud voice, "Lord, do not hold this sin against them." When he had said this, he died. (Acts 7:55–60).

Scripture tells us that this man Stephen, whom we honor as the first martyr, was able to follow our Lord in life, in death, and in generosity. Though he may not have known it at the time, it was the example of Stephen's death that gave courage to countless martyrs in the centuries of persecutions to come. And one young man in particular, who was present for Stephen's death, was profoundly affected by it. It was Saul of Tarsus, who later became our own St. Paul. In Paul's first encounter with Christianity, he saw it as a blasphemous perversion of the Jewish faith he cherished. He was first in line when it came to flushing out the followers of the Way and bringing them to "justice." He himself states, "You have heard, no doubt, of my earlier life in Judaism. I was violently persecuting the church of God and was trying to destroy it" (Galatians 1:13).

St. Stephen, then, was known for giving. He gave the Church the witness of his Spirit-filled life, the example of his courageous death, and the inspiration for all those who would follow. When your own gift-giving starts to feel burdensome this year, allow him to offer you the gift of perspective.

St. Stephen's Day is generally not observed in the United States, but it has long been a holy day in much of Europe. Time is spent with family, and the spirit of celebration continues with visits, gift-giving, singing, and conversation. Religious services in honor of Stephen can be found in certain countries, as well.

In England, Canada, Australia, New Zealand, and other parts of the Commonwealth, the 26th is also a secular holiday known as Boxing Day. The origins of this holiday are shrouded in a cloudy past, but essentially it was seen as a day to give gifts to the poor and needy. One legend tells of metal boxes being left outside churches, in which money and gifts could be placed for distribution. Another interpretation has the term originating with the gifts being put into boxes and wrapped in festive paper before being distributed to the poor.

In Ireland December 26 is known as Wren's Day, another traditional holiday whose origins are largely unclear. It is traditional on this day to hold a hunt, often for a wren (as legend held it was a wren that betrayed Stephen to the authorities). After the hunt families have potlucks with leftovers from their Christmas dinner. The day ends with celebrations at the pub, with entertainment and revelry lasting far into the night.

If Andrew is the saint who shows us how to begin, Stephen shows us how to end. Though a talented man noted for his character and leadership, he did not think of faith as one facet of his busy life. Rather he made it the center of his life, and his death. In so doing, he offered us a powerful example of courage and commitment.

What will your last Christmas look like? Could this be it? This Christmas, celebrate the season as though it were your last. One day, you'll be right.

CHAPTER NINE

The Feast of the Holy Family

CELEBRATING THE DOMESTIC CHURCH

Christ chose to be born and grow up in the bosom of the holy family of Joseph and Mary. The Church is nothing other than "the family of God." From the beginning, the core of the Church was often constituted by those who had become believers "together with all [their] household."... In our own time, in a world often alien and even hostile to faith, believing families are of primary importance as centers of living, radiant faith.[1]

Christmas is a time for family. We tend to pity those who spend the holidays alone—particularly if we ourselves are those people. One of the lessons of the Nativity story is that, despite the mystery surrounding Jesus' conception, despite having traveled far from home, despite grinding poverty, the little family at Bethlehem had one another. That's all anyone really needs to celebrate Christmas.

An oft-told story in homiletic circles is about an older woman who lived alone, rarely left her house, and suffered from depression. Hoping to encourage her to at least attend Mass, her pastor paid a visit. He walked her darkened rooms and noted photos of her deceased parents, her deceased husband, her children who never called. Most of the items in the woman's house were as neglected as she was, laboring under a film of dust and gloom. Grasping at straws, the pastor noted a couple of wilted African violets in one shadowy corner.

"I can tell you love flowers," he offered.

"Oh, yes," the woman agreed. "I used to love to garden…".

"Could you do me a favor?" the priest asked. We have a new family in the parish and I'd love to send them a little gift to welcome them. Do you think you could spare one of those plants?"

"I suppose so," the woman replied.

From that moment on, the pastor would greet the woman at Mass each week with a list of birth announcements, death announcements, First Communions, confirmations, weddings— you name it. For each occasion the now-very-busy woman supplied an African violet she had grown herself with a little note of condolence or well-wishing attached. First dozens, then hundreds of people in her community benefitted from her thoughtfulness and generosity.

Her funeral some years later was among the most-attended the parish had ever seen. Everyone came out to say good-bye to the "African violet lady."

Those of us blessed with family close by live each day with that consolation, but those who feel alone needn't despair. We need only look beyond ourselves to find someone—perhaps even a whole world—that needs our help. Our faith tells us that we are all children of one God. It is essential that we treat everyone—not just our blood relatives—as family. We might just find that we get the help we're looking for when we reach out and lend a helping hand to others first.

The *Catechism* talks of the family as a "domestic Church," recalling the house churches of the early Christians. The family is where most of us first learn the essentials of the faith and are brought up in the sacraments. Even for those who grew up in another faith or even without any family to speak of, our earliest years build into us ideas about good and evil, about the importance of loving and being loved. Many of us take years to find a place that truly feels like "home" or a group of loved ones that truly feel like "family." Those who have found both home and family in the Church are asked to extend some measure of that comfort and security to all those who are still seeking it for themselves.

Just how big is this family of God? The Church asks us to look beyond our human families to our churches, our communities, our nations—there's probably nothing earth-shattering in that idea. But it asks more, still. The Church asks that we go beyond our national borders, that we try to find the people least like us and find some common ground with them—that's a bit of a stretch for anyone. But it asks more, still. The Church asks that we think of the holy men and women who have gone before us—the communion of saints—and all those future generations that need our care and example—probably enough to keep us all very busy. The *Catechism* expresses this idea of Church in soaring language:

> "The eternal Father, in accordance with the utterly gratuitous and mysterious design of his wisdom and goodness, created the whole universe and chose to raise up men to share in his own divine life," to which he calls all men in his Son. "The Father…determined to call together in a holy Church those who should believe in Christ." This "family of God" is gradually formed and takes shape during the stages of human history, in keeping with the Father's plan. In fact, "already present in figure at the beginning of the world, this Church was prepared in marvelous fashion in the history of the people of Israel and the old Alliance. Established in this last age of the world and made manifest in the outpouring of the Spirit, it will be brought to glorious completion at the end of time."[2]

How does your family measure up to your ideal of what family should be? How do you measure up as a member of God's family? This Christmas, resolve to share a bit of home and family with someone who really needs it.

CHAPTER TEN

The Feast of the Epiphany

EAST MEETS WEST

The Epiphany is the manifestation of Jesus as Messiah of Israel, Son of God and Savior of the world. The great feast of Epiphany celebrates the adoration of Jesus by the wise men (magi) from the East, together with his baptism in the Jordan and the wedding feast at Cana in Galilee. In the magi, representatives of the neighboring pagan religions, the Gospel sees the first-fruits of the nations, who welcome the good news of salvation through the Incarnation. The magi's coming to Jerusalem in order to pay homage to the king of the Jews shows that they seek in Israel, in the messianic light of the star of David, the one who will be king of the nations.[1]

Although the traditional celebration of the Epiphany is January 6, this feast is now celebrated in the Church on the Sunday after Holy Family Sunday. It was the date that marked the end of the twelve days of Christmas—from December 25 through January 6—and remains for many the end of the Christmas celebration.

The Magi that arrive in Bethlehem on the Epiphany were from the East—quite likely Persia. Their interest in and knowledge of the stars, and the term *Magi* itself, makes it likely that they were priests of the cult of Zoroaster. Though Matthew doesn't say how many of these wise men made the famous trek, the number three seems to have derived from the fact that there were three gifts given to the Christ child: "On entering the house, they saw the child with Mary his mother; and they knelt down and paid him homage. Then, opening their treasure-chests, they offered him gifts of gold, frankincense, and myrrh" (2:11).

Two main traditions have formed around the meaning of the three gifts. One says that these gifts had royal significance, gifts given from kings to King. In this scenario, gold represents wealth, frankincense is a rich perfume, and myrrh an oil for anointing. The other theory is that the three gifts had a spiritual meaning: gold symbolized Jesus' virtue and his heavenly kingship; frankincense symbolized his priesthood; and myrrh symbolized his suffering and death.

Of what little we know of these travelers from afar, one thing is certain: They followed their own traditions in watching the stars and were led to Bethlehem, just as Herod's chief priests were able to advise him concerning the birth of the Messiah by consulting Scripture. It seems that all these methods lead to some sort of revelation. Does this suggest that all faiths are equal?

The Church is not willing to go that far. However, what it does teach is not quite the simplistic "outside the Church there is no salvation" that might have been familiar to our grandparents. The *Catechism* goes to some length to explain how we are to understand the value of the Catholic faith without being dismissive of the beliefs of others. It says:

> How are we to understand this affirmation, often repeated
> by the Church Fathers? Re-formulated positively, it means

that all salvation comes from Christ the Head through the Church which is his Body:

> Basing itself on Scripture and tradition, the Council teaches that the Church, a pilgrim now on earth, is necessary for salvation: the one Christ is the mediator and the way of salvation; he is present to us in his body which is the Church. He himself explicitly asserted the necessity of faith and Baptism, and thereby affirmed at the same time the necessity of the Church which men enter through Baptism as though a door. Hence they could not be saved who, knowing that the Catholic Church was founded as necessary by God through Christ, would refuse either to enter it or to remain in it.[2]

Thus, the Church teaches that we have a duty to know our faith and strive to live up to it once we're in it. If we're outside the faith, we have a duty to ask ourselves the "big questions" until we find the answers we seek. That's not quite the same as saying that you're either Catholic or condemned, though. The *Catechism* takes pains to add:

This affirmation is not aimed at those who, through no fault of their own, do not know Christ and his Church:

> Those who, through no fault of their own, do not know the Gospel of Christ or his Church, but who nevertheless seek God with a sincere heart, and, moved by grace, try in their actions to do his will as they know it through the dictates of their conscience—those too may achieve eternal salvation.[3]

In short, only God gets to decide who is saved and who is not. Our responsibility is to do our best to determine what God wants of us and then to do our best to fulfill that destiny, while allowing—even encouraging—others to follow their own path.

How can we celebrate the Feast of the Epiphany? In many Catholic parishes, chalk is distributed after Mass on Epiphany Sunday, and people are encouraged to go home and write above the main door of their house "20 + C + M + B + 12 "—that is, the number for the current decade, plus C for Caspar, M for Melchior, B for Balthasar, and the number for the current year (2012, in the example shown here). Some traditions hold that the letters C, M, and B also represent *Christus mansionem benedicat* (Christ bless this house).

In New Orleans, a ring-shaped cake known as a king cake is eaten anytime between the Epiphany and Mardi Gras. Within the cake is hidden a small, plastic figurine that represents the baby Jesus. Whoever gets the slice of cake with the Jesus figure must buy or bake the next cake. This custom is similar to one practiced in France, where the one who finds the hidden figure is crowned king for the day.

Have you ever been curious about another faith? Are you curious enough about your own? This Christmas, consider making a gift (to yourself or someone else) of a Catholic book or magazine.

The Baptism of Our Lord

A NEW BEGINNING

The baptism of Jesus is on his part the acceptance and inaugura-tion of his mission as God's suffering Servant. He allows himself to be numbered among sinners; he is already "the Lamb of God, who takes away the sin of the world." Already he is anticipating the "baptism" of his bloody death. Already he is coming to "fulfill all righteousness," that is, he is submitting himself entirely to his Father's will: out of love he consents to this baptism of death for the remission of our sins.[1]

The Feast of the Baptism of Our Lord marks the end of the Christmas season. Though baptism is usually the beginning of our life in faith, its presence at the end of the Christmas cycle has meaning. In every step of our journey, Christ has been there first. He has accepted being born as a frail human, to share in our sufferings and joys. He has consented to know what it means to lose friends (remember his tears at the death of Lazarus?), to watch his own mother suffer, to suffer himself the most gruesome torture and death. Whatever crosses we bear in our lives, we can be certain that Christ was there first.

His going before us has a deeper meaning as well. We are baptized *because* he was baptized and commands it of us. We accept our sufferings willingly *because* he accepted his willingly. We love him *because* he first loved us.

Our culture typically views the new year as the best time for new beginnings. Christmas and its memories are in the past, even if the tree is still with us. We're making resolutions, looking ahead to new opportunities, and resolving that *this* year, ah, this year....

Unlike some of our naysaying friends who will scoff at yet another attempt at self-improvement, Jesus believes in new beginnings. He counseled a frustrated Peter to forgive a trespassing brother not seven times in one day, but seventy-seven. He gave that same dear friend three chances to unsay his betrayal. And he gives us a fresh chance every day, every minute if we want it.

The Church teaches us that baptism is a once-for-all event. It washes us clean of sin, but if we've picked up a bit more along the way, there are no do-overs. For the clean-up work, the Church prescribes the sacrament of confession—also freely available, generally at convenient hours but, if you're desperate, pretty much at any time of day or night. Call your local parish and ask to talk to the priest: He'll make time for you.

In what area of your life do you need a new beginning, a fresh start? What events would you like to do over? This Christmas—this new year—start fresh in your relationship with Christ and his Church. Celebrate the new beginning that will make this, truly, a Catholic Christmas.

Notes

Introduction

1. *Catechism of the Catholic Church,* second edition (Vatican City: Libreria Editrice Vaticana, 1994, 1997), #642, quoting Galatians 4:4–5; Mark 1:1, 11; cf. Luke 1:55, 68. Quotes from the *Catechism* are hereinafter denoted by "CCC."

2. There is a fun discussion of all the Saturnalia celebrations at http://www.ancientsites.com/aw/ Article/70005.

Chapter One

1. CCC, #642, quoting 1 Corinthians 15:4–8; cf. Acts 1:22.

Chapter Two

1. CCC, #1168.

2. Fr. Thomas Richstatter, O.F.M., "The Liturgical Year: Simple Facts, Deep Truths," *Catholic Update,* December 2010.

3. J.L. Heilbron, *The Sun in the Church: Cathedrals as Solar Observatories* (Cambridge, Mass.: Harvard University Press, 1999), pp. 27–28.

4. William J. Broad, "How the Church Aided 'Heretical' Astronomy," *The New York Times,* October 19, 1999. See also www.webexhibits.org/calendars/year-astronomy.html.

Chapter Three

1. CCC, #858, quoting Mark 3:13–14; John 20:21, cf. 13:20; 17:18; Matthew 10:40; cf. Luke 10:16.

Chapter Four

1. *CCC*, #828, referencing *LG* 40, 48–51; John Paul II, *CL* 16, 3, *CL* 17, 3.

Chapter Five

1. *CCC*, #492, referencing *LG* 53, 56; cf. Ephesians 1:3–4.

Chapter Six

1. *CCC*, #736, quoting St. Basil, *De Spiritu Sancto*, 15, 36: PG 32, 132.

Chapter Seven

1. *CCC*, #462, quoting 1 John 4:2; 1 Timothy 3:16.

Chapter Eight

1. *CCC*, #2473, quoting St. Ignatius of Antioch, *Ad Rom.* 4,1: SCh 10, 110.

Chapter Nine

1. *CCC*, #1655–1656, referencing Acts 18:8.

2. *CCC*, #759, quoting *LG* 2.

Chapter Ten

1. *CCC*, #528, quoting Matthew 2:1; cf. *LH*, Epiphany, Evening Prayer II, Antiphon at the Canticle of Mary, cf. Matthew. 2:2; Numbers 24:17–19; Revelation 22:16; cf. John 4:22; Matthew 2:4–6.

2. *CCC*, #846, referencing Cyprian, Ep 73.21:PL 3, 1169; De unit.: *PL* 4 509–536, *LG* 14; cf. Mark 16:16; John 3:5.

3. *CCC*, #847, quoting *LG* 16; cf. *DS* 3866–3872.

Chapter Eleven

1. *CCC*, #536, quoting John 1:29, cf. Isaiah 53:12, cf. Mark 10:38; Luke 12:50; Matthew 3:15, cf. 26:39.

Bibliography

Catechism of the Catholic Church, second edition. Vatican City: Libreria Editrice Vaticana, 1994, 1997.

Catullus, Gaius Valerius. *Catullus, Tibullus, Pervigilium Veneris* (Loeb Classical Library No. 6). Cambridge, MA: Harvard University Press, 1988.

Grossman, John. *Christmas Curiosities: Odd, Dark, and Forgotten Christmas*. New York: Stewart, Tabori & Chang, 2008.

Heilbron, J.L. *The Sun in the Church: Cathedrals as Solar Observatories*. Cambridge, MA: Harvard University Press, 1999.

Kelly, Joseph F. *The Origins of Christmas*. Collegeville, MN: Liturgical, 2004.

Klauser, Theodor. *A Short History of the Western Liturgy*. New York: Oxford University Press, 1979.

Metzger, Marcel. *History of the Liturgy: The Major Stages*. Collegeville, MN: Liturgical, 1997.

Nissenbaum, Stephen. *The Battle for Christmas*. New York: Vintage, 1997.

Richstatter, Thomas. O.F.M. "The Liturgical Year: Simple Facts, Deep Truths," *Catholic Update*, December 2010.

Walsh, Michael, ed. *Butler's Lives of the Saints*. San Francisco: HarperSanFrancisco, 1991.